REAL WORLD ECONOMICS™

How
Inflation
Works

Joyce Hart

+6.73
+1.33
+9.19
+11.02

+21.64
+14.83
+3.24
+32.47
+2.35
+.41
+.21
+2.42
+5.53

ROSEN
PUBLISHING®
New York

Published in 2010 by The Rosen Publishing Group, Inc.
29 East 21st Street, New York, NY 10010

First Edition

Library of Congress Cataloging-in-Publication Data

Hart, Joyce, 1954–
How inflation works / Joyce Hart.
    p. cm.—(Real world economics)
Includes bibliographical references and index.
ISBN-13: 978-1-4358-5320-1 (library binding)
1. Inflation (Finance)—Juvenile literature. I. Title.
HG229.H2597 2009
332.4'1—dc22

                                                            2008047679

Manufactured in the United States of America

CPSIA Compliance Information: Batch #BR902021YA: For futher information contact Windmill Books, New York, New York at 1-866-478-0556.

On the cover: In 2008, the plummeting stock market, credit and mortgage crises, and sharp decreases in spending and consumer confidence all made headlines as a worldwide recession took strong hold. These troubling developments had a silver lining—earlier fears of an inflation evaporated as the money supply shrank.

Contents

INTRODUCTION

If you own a bike or have decorated your house for a birthday party, you should be familiar with one version of the word "inflation." If your bike tire becomes flat, you use inflation to fill it with air so you can take a ride. If you use balloons to decorate for a party, you also use inflation to make the balloons big. Inflation is an expansion or an increase. When you pump up your flat bicycle tire, it enlarges. When you blow into a skinny balloon, it becomes nice and fat.

Inflation in the economy is somewhat similar. There is also an expansion or increase. This increase is most easily seen in the rise of the cost of living. Inflation, in terms of economics, refers to a continuing rise in the general price level of goods and services. In other words, when there is inflation, the cost of food is higher than it was the year before. It requires more money to fill the gas tank of the family car. Buying your favorite compact disks or downloaded songs costs more. And although you have been saving your money for that pair of jeans you saw at the

store last winter, this winter those jeans might be out of your price range if there is high inflation.

Under some conditions, inflation is good. Inflation helps to boost profits for the people who make goods. This, in turn, helps the economy because those profits might be reinvested. For example, if a business makes extra money, the owners might share those profits with their employees. So one day, your mom or dad might come home and say, "I got a raise." This means he or she is now making more money. To celebrate, your parents might go out and buy a new car or invest in a new computer and a new library of computer games. When your parents—and other people in your community and around the country—purchase new items, the stores from which they bought those goods also celebrate. They are making more money, too.

If inflation is not controlled, however, the economy can suffer. If prices on goods continue to rise, and your parents' salaries do not increase, then new cars, new computers, and even food can

Inflation means that the pair of jeans you wanted last year costs more money this year.

cost more money than some people can afford. Their income, or earnings, are not keeping up with inflation.

Many economists believe that a healthy rate of inflation is around a 3 percent increase each year. This means that

prices rise from one year to the next at a rate of 3 percent, or three pennies per dollar spent. So, if it costs you $10 to rent a Wii game this year, next year that same game would cost $10.30 to rent. A 3 percent rise in inflation is not difficult to handle for most people who are employed (have a job). Most likely, many of them receive raises every year, which helps to offset a 3 percent inflation hike on the cost of goods.

There are ways of controlling inflation, which will be discussed in later chapters. But to give you an example of how this might work in your own life, let's look at a hypothetical (make-believe) situation.

Suppose you had a friend named Scott whose family owned a lemon orchard. In the summer, Scott set up a lemonade stand and sold some of the best lemonade you ever tasted. You and all your neighbors looked forward to seeing Scott at his stand, and you all bought tall glasses of lemonade faster than Scott could make it. So this year, Scott decided to raise the price from $1 to $2 per glass. The first time you went to his stand, you were shocked by this

The cost of gasoline rose dramatically in 2008, as did food prices, raising fears that the nation was entering an inflationary period.

inflated price. However, you were very thirsty, so you paid the extra dollar.

But as the summer went along, you and your neighbors started complaining about the extra money that Scott was charging. No one could afford the new high price, so everyone stopped going to Scott's stand. Scott sat there all day waiting for people to come by, but no one did. All the lemonade he had made went bad, and he had to throw it away. This went on for a week. Eventually, Scott figured it out. He finally realized that he had to lower his price to lure his customers back to his stand. Scott put up new signs, advertising that the price had been cut in half. He was once again selling lemonade at a price of $1 per glass. You and your neighbors, who were eager to drink the greatest lemonade in the world, almost ran back to Scott's stand. Soon, Scott's business was once again thriving.

Economies of large countries like the United States are not quite as simple as Scott's lemonade stand. However, some of the same economic principles are used by the federal govern-ment to help control various kinds of inflation. The government wants to make sure that inflation does not get out of control. There is a constant monitoring of the economy to make sure that goods (like food and gasoline) and services (like hospitals and public transportation) are affordable. In other words, the economy of a country works best when people are making enough money to buy the things they need and want. Therefore, the government makes adjustments so that businesses can remain successful, while at the same time making it possible for people to afford to buy their goods.

CHAPTER ONE

Defining Inflation and Identifying Its Causes

Economists usually talk about the definition of inflation in the same breath as they talk about its causes. The two are indistinguishable, with "types" of inflation and "causes" of inflation often being interchangeable.

Identifying Inflation

Inflation is more than just an increase in the cost of goods and services. For economists to declare that a country's economy is indeed in a state of inflation, the cost of food, gasoline, and other important goods that people need have to not only rise significantly, but this rise also has to last over a relatively long period of time.

What this means is that the price of a movie ticket might increase from $6 to $9 over a period of two years, but this does not necessarily mean that the economy is suffering the effects of inflation. This might just mean that the owner of the movie theater wants to make a bigger profit. A profit is the extra

When the cost of grocery store items rises, people might be forced to buy less food or food of lower quality.

money a business owner makes after all expenses have been paid. The theater owner might be betting that enough people want to see movies badly enough that they will pay the extra money for tickets. The price he charges rises even though his operating expenses have not risen at the same rate. So, his price increase is a profit-driven choice he makes, rather than something he has to do to stay in business. If, however, the owner has raised ticket prices to cover his own increasing costs of doing business, and ticket prices remain high for a long period of time, this would be a symptom of inflation.

Economists identify inflation in different ways. One of the ways is to calculate how much purchasing (or buying) power consumers are enjoying. For example, economists might measure if $50 buys as much food today as it did two years ago. If their research finds that the answer to this question is that $50 buys just as much today as it did two years ago, then there is no inflation in the food market. But they might not end their research there. They might ask other questions. Does $50 buy as much gasoline as it did two years ago? They might examine the price of clothing or how much it costs to visit a doctor. If they find significant price increases in any of the major goods or services, then they analyze the results further. They will want to know how big the price increases are and how these increases are affecting families. Even if food prices are not inflated, the inflated costs of other goods and services might be causing families serious financial difficulties.

Going Off the Gold Standard

Although the U.S. currency used to be backed by gold or silver, this is no longer true. Today, the U.S. currency's worth is based on the potential wealth of the country. In other words, the worth of U.S. currency depends on the money that American citizens and businesses will make in the future and on the taxes on that income and wealth that they will pay to the government. The U.S. currency, therefore, has worth not in and of itself (it's only paper), but rather because it symbolizes wealth and can be used to trade for goods and services. The U.S. dollar, in other words, has become a medium of exchange. U.S. money can be used to exchange goods and services, but you can no longer go to a bank with a $10 bill and ask for the $10 worth of gold that once backed that bill.

Another term that economists use in reference to inflation is "hyperinflation." In 2008, Zimbabwe was suffering an inflation rate of over 2 million percent. Economists call this hyperinflation because Zimbabwe's inflation was rising unusually fast. Hyperinflation most often occurs when a government prints too much money, which is one of the things that was happening in Zimbabwe. The more money that a government prints, the less value that money has. The less value that money has, the higher the prices rise because greater amounts of the less valuable currency are needed to buy things.

Devalued Currency

As a practical example of how devalued currency works, imagine that you own one of the rarest cards in the whole Pokémon series. What would you be willing to trade for this rare card? Now, imagine that everyone just learned that this rare card you own has been duplicated by the company that makes Pokémon cards. Now, instead of there being just 100 cards in the world, there are 100 million of them. Because the company has made so many copies of this once-rare card, the value of your Pokémon card has just been devalued. It is now far less valuable than it was when it was rare. In comparison with how many cards you once might have requested in exchange for trading your rare card, the value of your card has now been greatly diminished. You will receive much fewer cards in a trade for it.

This same procedure works with a nation's currency. Paper money is valued because of standards that a country sets for those paper bills. For instance, let's pretend that there is a country that has a paper currency called the "dangle." That country prints 10,000 dangle bills made of paper. The paper is

Inflation often makes people think twice about spending their money. This means stores make less money and may be forced to lay off workers.

not worth anything by itself. However, if the country guarantees that one dangle stands for one ounce of silver and that same country promises that it has 10,000 ounces of silver available in its bank, then a paper dangle is worth something. One dangle is worth one ounce of silver.

But one year later, let's say that the government wants to increase its currency (wants to make more money), so it prints 10,000 more dangles. Unfortunately, that same country does not have 10,000 more ounces of silver to back up this new printing of paper dangles. So, the 10,000 paper dangles plus the original 10,000 dangles are not worth an ounce of silver each. They are now worth only one-half an ounce of silver. Although a citizen of this country might have been able to buy a bike for one dangle last year, that same bike now costs two dangles. Imagine how much less a dangle would be worth if the government had printed one million more dangles without increasing the amount of silver in its bank to back up the currency. This is one of the causes of hyperinflation, and it is exactly what has happened in Zimbabwe.

Causes of Inflation

Just as inflation might be identified in a variety of ways, there are also different causes of inflation, including an increase in the demand for a product and an increase in production costs.

Demand-Pull Inflation

Demand-pull inflation occurs when a lot of people in households, the government, businesses, or foreign countries want to buy something, but there are not enough goods or services available. Let's go back to Scott's lemonade stand to understand how an increase in demand can result in higher prices.

It was a hard winter for Scott's parents' orchard. A late winter frost killed many of the lemons. So in the spring and summer months, when Scott's neighbors came to Scott's lemonade stand, they found only one pitcher of lemonade. Scott sold ten glasses of lemonade, but there were fifteen people who stood in line. This means that five people went home without tasting the lemonade.

Those five people who did not get the lemonade the first day rushed to Scott's stand very early the next morning. They

When supply of a certain popular item, like the newest version of PlayStation, is low, demand is usually high. This causes a demand-pull inflation and a rise in prices.

wanted to make sure they would be first in line for the new batch of juice that Scott was making. The news had gotten out that there was only a small supply of lemonade this year. So another twenty people came running to Scott's stand, too, hoping to get a taste of the lemonade before the supply completely ran out. Again, Scott had only enough lemonade for ten people. So, fifteen people went home without tasting the sweet drink.

On the third day, even more people showed up at the stand. There was some pushing and shoving going on for the first ten places in line. Scott realized that his lemonade was in high demand. People really wanted his lemonade. He wondered what would happen if he changed his price from $1 per glass to $2 per glass. He soon found out. Some people left because they refused to pay the 100 percent inflated price. But ten people paid the doubled price, and Scott made a big profit.

In this example, the demand for the lemonade pulled the price up, causing the inflation. This type of inflation often happens in business, especially when a new product, such as the long-awaited Nintendo electronic game player Wii, first come out on the market. So many people wanted to buy the Wii that Nintendo could not keep up with the demand. So, the price of the Wii remained high. Once most of the orders for the Wii were met and not as many people wanted to buy it, then the company lowered the price to encourage more reluctant or less enthusiastic consumers to buy it.

Cost-Push Inflation

Cost-push inflation occurs when a company's costs go up. This might be caused by a variety of incidents, such as having to pay higher taxes or higher salaries or experiencing an increase in the cost of supplies that are needed to make the company's products.

For example, let's say that Scott had three major new costs before he opened his lemonade stand this year. First, the wood in Scott's old stand rotted, and he had to build a new stand. The wood was expensive, costing him $30. Second, last year he received a notice from the city, stating that he would have to buy a permit that gave him the city's permission to sell lemonade on the street. The permit cost Scott $15. Third, last summer some people had complained that the lemonade was too warm. Scott's customers asked if they could have some ice in the lemonade. So, Scott bought a cooler to keep the ice in. This cost him another $15. Scott had extra costs this year that amounted to $60.

In order to make as much money as he did last year, Scott calculated that he would have to raise the cost of each glass of lemonade to $1.50. The extra costs that Scott had to pay for the new supplies and the permit "pushed up" the need for the inflated price of lemonade.

Cost-push inflation often occurs in a business when its workers' salaries, production and supply costs, and other expenses are higher than the amount of money that the owner can make in selling the business's goods or services.

A good example of this is the airline business. Airlines sell the service of transportation. Pilots, who fly the planes, need to be well trained and experienced. In order to attract the best pilots, an airline has to pay them a good salary. In 2008, when the price of gasoline doubled, the airline business had to pay a lot more money to buy supplies (expensive gasoline to

Because of the steep rise in gasoline prices in 2008, the cost of airline tickets also rose. This type of inflation is called cost-push inflation.

fuel the planes). In order to pay for these fuel and personnel costs, the airlines raised the cost of airline tickets. They also added extra charges for checking in suitcases, for using pillows and blankets, and for drinking beverages (which used to be free). These extra charges helped the airlines cover their costs. The higher prices for the airline tickets were the result of cost-push inflation.

CHAPTER TWO
The History of Currency and Inflation

Throughout history, as long as goods and services required payment, the price of things people needed could rise and fall. These price swings depended on how big the supply was and how many people demanded the goods.

Before there was a form of money, people used to barter for goods and services. This means that people would make deals with one another and then swap one set of goods or services for another. For example, a goat herder might barter with a farmer by offering goats' milk or goats' cheese in exchange for the farmer's corn or wheat. A tailor might offer to make a new suit of clothes for a livestock owner in exchange for a horse.

If there were a lot of farmers in one village who raised chickens that produced more eggs than the villagers could eat, then the value of the eggs might be fairly low. But if there was just one cobbler in the village, he could demand a lot of goods in exchange for a new pair of shoes that he knew how to make. If the value (the worth) of a product is low, so too is its price.

Before countries created currency systems, or money, people obtained goods and services by bartering, or trading.

If something is highly valued, it costs more. The price of something reflects what it is worth, or how highly it is valued.

As time went by and the populations of towns began to grow, pulling a horse all over town or chasing a herd of sheep through the city streets to use as barter became more difficult and inconvenient. So, bartering was not always the best, most efficient way to purchase goods or services. This is when money came into use. But money did not always take the form of coins and paper bills as it does today. In fact, one kind of early money took the form of seashells.

Shells and Metal Coins as Money

In many ancient cultures, such as in Africa, China, India, and North America before the arrival of Europeans, shells were prized possessions. Shells were used just as people use money today. The shells were different from one culture to another, but they all worked in the same way. Everything that a person might need could be exchanged for a certain number of shells.

It wasn't until later, sometime around 3000 BCE, that gold was first used as money. At first, gold nuggets were used. The nuggets had to be weighed during each transaction to guarantee their worth. The more the nugget weighed, the more it was worth. Then, over time, instead of using gold nuggets of random weights, the gold was melted into the form of bars that had a uniform weight. Using gold bars as a form of money was more convenient that pulling a wagon of chickens into town, but gold bars were heavy and still not as portable as modern forms of money are.

Many years later, silver was added as a prized currency. Sometimes gold and silver were made in the form of rings that

Ancient countries at one time used precious metals, like these Roman gold bars, for money.

could be worn on a person's fingers or carried on leather strings. People used the gold and silver rings like we use coins and paper money today.

During the seventh century BCE, the gold and silver that were used as money were made into coins. The first coins were made in Asia Minor (in the area of modern-day Turkey). About this same time, China also developed metal coins. But the coins were not all made of gold and silver. Other metals, such as bronze, copper, and tin, were also used by ancient cultures. For a while, China even used leather coins.

Coins were also used by the Greeks and the Romans, who mixed cheaper metals in with their gold and silver coins when they needed more money. The less gold and silver in the coins, the less value the coins had. Mixing in cheaper metals in order to be able to make more coins is the same as today's practice of printing more money without having any additional value to back the new bills. Just like in modern economies, the Greeks and the Romans suffered from inflation when they devalued the coins in this way. As the coins lost value (because they were no longer made of pure gold or silver), more coins were needed to purchase goods and services. That was when inflation set in.

The Development of Paper Money

The Chinese were the first to issue paper money, around 806 CE. They created paper bills because they were running low on copper, the main metal they used for their coins. Their paper bills were based on real worth and were backed by reserves of precious metals in banks. As in other countries, however, when the Chinese people needed more money, they just printed more paper bills and no longer backed the bills with the same amount of real wealth (such as gold). The paper money began to lose its worth. As in so many instances in which countries increased their money supply without maintaining its worth, inflation in China soared.

The American colonies created their own form of money. When it came time to go up against Great Britain during the Revolutionary War (1775-1783), the Continental Congress (the governing body of the original thirteen colonies/states before and during the war) produced paper money called Continentals. At first, the Congress promised that the Continentals would be backed by silver. However, as the war dragged on, the army's expenses grew, and the Congress printed Continentals far beyond the amount of silver they had to back them. By the end of the war, the paper money was almost worthless. This flooding of the economy with lots of money that had little or no real worth caused severe inflation.

Although paper money was used in Europe and in the North American colonies in earlier centuries, it wasn't until 1816 that a gold standard was set for the paper bills. The government in England was the first to set gold as the standard value backing paper money. It did this to stop the inflation that had arisen due to banks printing paper money and randomly setting its value, rather than backing the value on actual gold or silver. Most early paper money was more like a promise from the bank that the bills could be exchanged for a certain amount of precious metal. But the banks offered no guarantee that this would actually happen before the gold standard was made the rule.

A $50 bill from colonial America depicts Atlas shouldering a heavy burden on his powerful shoulders.

With the gold standard established in England, each banknote (the paper money) had a specific value in gold. In 1900, the United States passed the Gold Standard Act, which meant that paper money in America would also be backed by gold.

Today, the gold standard no longer exists in either Europe or the United States. Instead, the U.S. dollar is based on the potential wealth of the country and the performance of the U.S. economy relative to other countries. American citizens and businesses must pay taxes, for instance, and those taxes become the basis of some of the country's potential wealth. So, as long as the U.S. economy is doing well, the U.S. dollar is considered strong. But when the economy is not doing well—when the country's potential to generate wealth decreases—the U.S. dollar loses its strength. In general, the dollar is worth less during economic downturns than it is during boom times.

Because all currencies around the world are not based on the same gold standard, or are not based on any gold standard at all, the worth of a country's currency constantly rises and falls, depending on how well the country's economy is doing.

Wartime Inflation in the United States

One of the first serious occurrences of inflation in the United States was the result of the Revolutionary War. As stated before, the Continental Congress, instead of raising taxes to pay for the war, authorized multiple increases in the amount of paper money to be printed to finance the war. But the Congress did not back the increased amount of currency with additional amounts of real worth (such as gold or silver). As

During the Civil War, the Confederate Southern states printed their own money. Various Confederate bills from several Southern states appear above.

a result, there was inflation. Inflation often occurs when a country is waging war. The country prints a lot of extra money to pay its bills and to buy military equipment and supplies. By the end of the war, everyone knows that the money is

not backed by real wealth, so the currency becomes worthless. This also happened during the Civil War, when the Southern states printed their own Confederate money. At the war's end, when the Confederacy no longer existed, the Confederate money had no worth at all.

Wartime inflation is not always due to the government printing more dollar bills than it has actual wealth in the form of silver and gold reserves. Sometimes a government borrows money from another country. When the war is over, that government has to pay back the money it borrowed plus extra money for the interest charged on the loan. When someone loans money, they usually charge the person who is borrowing the money interest.

Interest is a percentage of the money that is borrowed. So, if you borrowed $10 from a bank, the bank might charge you 10 percent interest. This means that you would have to pay back the $10 you borrowed plus the interest, which would be an additional dollar. You would owe the bank $11, even though you borrowed only $10.

A store display during World War II asks customers to help fight inflation by buying goods that are priced especially low.

Now, imagine if a country borrowed several million dollars. Or, what if a country borrowed billions of dollars? Ten percent interest on just $1 million would be $100,000. What this means is that by the end of a war, a government might owe a bank or another country so much money that it has trouble paying it off. The government might then have to raise taxes on things like gasoline and cigarettes to collect more money to pay back the loan. Higher taxes, in turn, mean that goods and services now cost more money. And that means inflation.

Inflation hit the U.S. economy especially hard during such conflicts as the Civil War, World Wars I and II, the Korean War, and the Vietnam War. During World War II, the price of

Comparison of Approximate Cost of Living from 1950s to 2000s

	1950s	1980s	2008
Movie ticket	$0.50	$3.50	$8
McDonald's hamburger	$0.15	$0.50	$0.89
Chocolate candy bar	$0.05	$0.25	$1
Loaf of bread	$0.16	$0.51	$2.50
Postage stamp	$0.03	$0.20	$0.42
Average house	$16,000	$100,000	$250,000
Average car	$1,800	$6,000	$20,000
Average gallon of gas	$0.20	$1	$4
Average salary	$3,000	$16,000	$50,000
Average annual tuition at a four-year private college	$1,000	$5,000	$15,000

goods rose at a 7 percent rate of inflation. During World War I, at times, prices rose over 200 percent.

After World War II, with a few exceptions, inflation in the U.S. economy was kept fairly low. The inflation rate for most

The demand for gasoline in the 1970s was so great—and the supply sometimes so low—that gas stations often ran out of fuel.

of the postwar years to the mid-2000s averaged about 3 percent. Many economists believe that an inflation rate around 3 percent is good for the economy. A 3 percent inflation rate provides healthy profits for businesses, while allowing most

people salary increases that can keep up with a moderately rising cost of living. There were higher peaks of inflation, however, such as during the Korean War in the 1950s, when inflation was at 5.9 percent. Also, while America was becoming mired in the Vietnam War during the 1960s and early 1970s, prices in the United States rose at a 5.7 percent rate.

Inflation and Fuel Prices

During the 1970s, American citizens saw inflation rates rise even more significantly. In some years of the decade, inflation rose as high as 13 percent. Some of this high inflation was due to the ongoing Vietnam War. Another reason for the high inflation of the 1970s, however, was due to very high oil prices. The oil-producing nations of the Middle East cut back on the production of oil. This created a high demand for an increasingly limited supply of oil. Americans were soon spending hours in long lines that stretched for blocks at gas stations, waiting to fill their gas tanks. Many gas stations ran out of gas before everyone could fill their tanks. So, people would drive to another gas station or come back to the same station the next day. Eventually, people were assigned days they could show up at a gas station.

This scarcity (lack of supply) created high demand for gasoline, so fuel prices kept rising and quickly became inflated. The gas station owners were forced to pay more money to the companies that produced and supplied the gasoline. Then, in order to make up for the extra money they were paying to fuel producers and suppliers, the gas station owners charged more for the gas that people pumped into their cars.

In 2008, the price of gasoline also rose sharply. The inflation rate for fuel was much higher than the increase in people's salaries. While, in the years prior to 2008, people might have paid $30 to fill up their gas tank, they were now paying $60 or more. When the price of gasoline goes up, so too does the price of food. Farmers, who produce the food, use gasoline to run their tractors and other farm machinery. They also use gasoline to haul their crops to the market.

Farmers pass these extra costs onto the stores that buy their produce and the food processors who use their grain, produce, and meat. And the stores and food processors pass the extra costs onto consumers who buy the food for their families. In times of higher fuel prices, therefore, families are not only spending more money to fill up their cars with gasoline and heat their homes with oil or natural gas, they are also spending more money on food.

High oil prices also affect businesses. The goods that a business purchases are sometimes transported to its store by large commercial barges that bring the goods across the ocean. Freight trains with diesel engines transport a large percentage of goods, too. Some goods are brought in by air. Then, trucks are used to bring the goods from the airports and the docks. Everyone along the way pays the high cost of fuel. Everyone passes these costs on. So, the store pays more for the goods and passes the extra costs onto the consumer. This means that when you go to the store, you pay more for clothing, games, books, and school supplies.

CHAPTER THREE
Measuring Inflation

The U.S. federal government, through the Department of Labor, measures inflation as best it can. It is not a perfect system of measurement because products cost more in some cities than they do in others. Also, the government only looks at the cost of living that people in a city or urban environment experience. Nevertheless, the information that the Department of Labor collects provides a solid sense of what is going on in the economy.

The Department of Labor collects the information and then produces what is called the consumer price index (CPI). There are other, similar collections of economic information, but the CPI is the index that is used the most often. The CPI is used to gauge the average change, over time, of what people are spending on goods and services. The department does this by selecting specific goods and services that are routinely bought by consumers. The people who are chosen for the survey are asked to list the goods and services that they buy and how much they pay for them.

So-called big box stores like Wal-Mart buy huge amounts of goods at a discount so they can beat inflation and offer their customers lower prices.

The CPI Market Basket

The Department of Labor collects information about the buying patterns of people who live in metropolitan (city) areas. They send surveys to urban consumers and urban wage earners. This group, according to the Department of Labor, represents about 87 percent of the entire population of the United States. The department also sends surveys to people who are unemployed, people who are self-employed (people who run their own businesses), and people who are retired. People who live in rural areas of the country, such as farming families, and people who are in the military are not included in the surveys.

37

It is from this information that the Department of Labor creates what it calls a market basket. This market basket is not a real basket. It is a representation of the most popular items—almost 80,000 goods and services—that people in the United States pay for each year.

To create the market basket, the Department of Labor asks about 60,000 families from around the country to keep a list of what they have bought during a three-month period. The department also asks another 28,000 families to keep a daily diary of what they purchase during a two-week period. The Department of Labor then takes these reports and studies the goods and services that are listed. It gives certain items that appear frequently more importance than others that only appear infrequently. The next step is to choose the most important items. It is these most frequently purchased goods and services that are put into the market basket.

The market basket items fall into several distinct categories. These categories are:

Food and beverages—This includes goods such as cereals, milk, coffee, chicken, wine, and snacks.

Housing—This includes the money people pay for rent, oil or natural gas to heat the home, and furniture.

Clothing—This includes the clothes men, women, and children wear, as well as jewelry.

Transportation—This includes new and used cars, fares for airlines, mass transit, gasoline, and car insurance.

Medical care—This includes doctor visits, stays in hospitals, medications, eyeglasses, and other medical services.

Other Ways of Measuring Inflation

The consumer price index is just one way to measure inflation. The CPI measures inflation from the point of view of consumers, the people who buy things. There is another index called the producer price index (PPI). The PPI measures inflation from the point of view of

The costs of all goods imported into the United States are studied as part of the International Price Program and its attempts to monitor inflation.

the people who make the products. Inflation is also measured by the employment cost index (ECI), which measures inflation from the point of view of the labor market (the workers). The Department of Labor uses its Bureau of Labor Statistics' International Price Program to measure inflation by studying the products that the United States imports (buys from other countries) and exports (products made in the United States and sent to other countries). There is also a study called the Gross Domestic Product Deflator, which measures inflation both by what consumers buy as well as what the government spends.

Recreation—This includes television, sports equipment, pets and pet supplies, and things like movie tickets.

Education and communication—This includes college tuition, telephone services, and computer software.

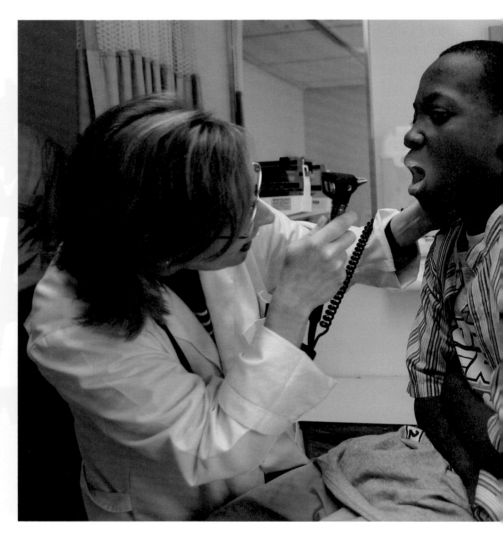

The cost of this teenager's visit to a doctor could cost almost one hundred times more than when his grandfather was his age.

Other goods and services—This includes things such as cigarettes, haircuts, funeral expenses, and other personal services.

There are additional items that the Department of Labor includes, such as taxes people pay when they buy certain goods and services and money spent on things like water and sewage bills. Items that are not included are taxes on people's wages (income tax) or money that people spend on investments (like stocks and bonds), real estate (land and houses or apartments), or life insurance.

Analyzing Market Basket Data

The Department of Labor has workers who either visit or call thousands of stores, manufacturers, service providers (such as doctors' and dentists' offices), and other places of business to collect as much information about goods and services as they can. They gather information about the prices being charged as well as how many products are selling. These workers, called economic assistants, record the prices of about 80,000 different items each month. They not only collect the prices of items, they also register the sizes of cans and bottles that contain some of the products being

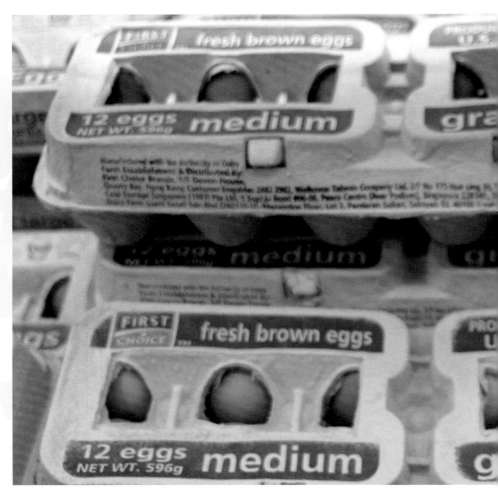

Eggs are a staple item—a basic necessity—whose rising cost would have an important impact on a family's finances. These "bread and butter" kinds of items are part of the market basket data studied by the government to come up with the consumer price index.

sold. The reason they do this is so the price recorded is as accurate as possible.

For example, an economic assistant named Anna noticed that a can of soda cost $1.50 last year and that the same soda still costs $1.50 this year. However, Anna thought the can of soda looked different. So she checked the amount of soda in the can and discovered that the company that made the soda had changed the size of the can. The can last year held eight ounces. But this year, the can holds only six ounces. So, even though the price is still $1.50, the consumer is buying less soda. If you pay the same amount of money for a smaller can, you are actually paying more because the same amount of money buys you less soda.

Another detail that economic assistants look for is a change in value. Let's say that last year a dozen eggs cost $1.45. This year, a dozen eggs cost $2.50. Does this mean that the price is inflated? Or has something in addition to price changed? This time Anna, the economic assistant, reads

the label on the egg carton. She finds that the same company that sold a dozen eggs last year for $1.45 has switched from selling regular eggs to selling certified organic eggs. In order to sell certified organic eggs, the egg farmer has to put more money into his chickens, by feeding them better food and providing them with more space, for instance. The customer who buys the certified organic eggs is getting a better product than if he or she bought regular eggs. When a consumer gets better quality (healthier eggs in this case), he or she expects to pay more money. So, the rise in the price of eggs was not caused by inflation.

All of the information that economic assistants collect is sent back to the Department of Labor. There, specialists in economics and commodities (commodities are products that people buy) study and analyze it. These specialists make sure that the economic assistants have not made any mistakes. Once all the information has been verified as correct, the consumer price index is created. The prices of the items in the market basket are compared to similar market basket data from previous years. The specialists compare the baskets from one year to the next to see if overall prices are going up, remaining the same, or going down. It is from this comparison that the specialists decide if the economy is leaning toward inflation, is stagnant (remaining the same), or is experiencing deflation.

CHAPTER FOUR

The Effects of Inflation

E conomists state that whether inflation helps or hurts you depends on a complex set of circumstances and situations.

The Benefits of a Low Inflation Rate

The first circumstance to look at is the rate of inflation. Normally, if inflation is between 2 and 3 percent, economists tend to agree that this is a good thing. An inflation rate at this level demonstrates that the economy is growing. Businesses are making profits because most people can afford to buy goods and services. These profits are then put back into the businesses so they can create new products, which grab the attention of even more consumers. Businesses might even offer their employees better wages. This makes their employees happy and also encourages their workers to go out and purchase new goods and services, too. So, you can see how an inflation rate of 2 or 3 percent can help a growing economy grow even healthier.

Let's visit Scott and his lemonade stand again. One day, Scott decided to raise the cost of his lemonade from $1 a glass to $1.03 (a 3 percent increase). Not many people would complain about this inflated price. Another three cents is fairly easy

Apple's iPhone is another example of a consumer good whose relatively low supply was met with huge demand, resulting in long lines at the stores that sold it and many unlucky, empty-handed customers.

to adjust to. Over the course of the summer, this extra three cents per glass gave Scott an additional $6 profit from the two lemonade stands that he operated.

The next summer, Scott bought three pints of strawberries

with his $6 profit from the previous year. Then, he advertised that he had a new product. His customers could buy his regular lemonade for $1.03, as usual. But his new product, strawberry lemonade, would cost them $1.25 per glass. Not everyone wanted to pay extra for the strawberry lemonade, though the new product sounded delicious. But some people did try the strawberry lemonade and loved it. Scott loved it, too. Whereas the regular lemonade gave him a $6 profit at the end of the summer, the strawberry lemonade was popular enough that it also provided him with an additional $6 profit, despite being more expensive to make.

Under these conditions, Scott obviously benefited from the inflation of his prices. He was able to improve the variety of his drinks, and he could give his cousin (who worked the second lemonade stand) an extra $2 for helping him. Scott's customers also benefited. They were able to enjoy Scott's original lemonade with only a three cent increase. The extra money that they paid inspired Scott to invest

When inflation rises steeply, money is suddenly worth much less than it used to be. As a result, it can buy much less than it used to.

in strawberries and create a new drink, one that was enjoyed by a large number of his old customers and that attracted some new customers.

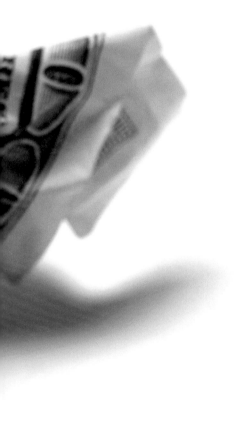

How High Inflation Can Be Harmful

A 3 percent inflation rate is considered a sign of economic health. But if inflation goes higher than 3 percent, a wide range of people may begin to suffer. A 10 percent inflation rate, for instance, would raise the price of Scott's original lemonade to $1.13 per glass. Some people could afford this inflated price because the money they make might have also increased. But the 10 percent hike in price might be too high for other people. Some people, like the retired and elderly, live on a fixed income. That means they receive the same amount of money each year, without any raises. Their income does not keep up with the inflation rate, so what they can spend each year decreases as prices increase.

Here's an example of how a 10 percent inflation rate might hurt someone. Alan receives an allowance of $10 a week. He has received this same amount ever since he turned twelve years old. Alan is now fourteen. In the past two years, inflation has increased the prices of most of the things he likes to buy by 10 percent. Since his allowance has not increased at all, Alan's $10 is actually worth only $8 now. He can buy only $8 worth of goods with his weekly allowance because the 10 percent inflation has deflated the real worth of his allowance. So, when Alan walks by Scott's lemonade stand, he has to think twice about buying a glass of the juice. He wants to buy a new baseball cap, so he is a little worried about whether he will have enough money for both the cap and the lemonade. The baseball cap he wants cost $8 last year. With the 10 percent inflation, that would increase the price to $8.80 without taxes. Alan decides not to buy the lemonade.

If there are a lot of people living on fixed incomes, like Alan, Scott will have fewer customers coming to his stand once prices start to rise. If fewer people buy Scott's lemonade, he might have to lower his prices so that people will be more willing to purchase it. If Scott has to lower his price, he will not make enough profit to give his cousin the extra $2 that he gave him the previous year. Also, Scott will not have enough profit to buy the strawberries and will have to stop offering his popular and profitable strawberry lemonade special.

Inflation, Spending, and Personal Financial Planning

Many parents put money into a savings account for their children's future college costs. Most parents even make adjustments for an inflated cost of college tuition in the future. For instance, the Millers have a ten-year-old daughter. They know that in eight years, their daughter may want to go to the University of Washington. In 2008, the cost of classes alone (no dorm room, books, or food included in this cost) was about $16,000 a year, or $64,000 for the entire four years of college. The Millers anticipate a normal, relatively low annual increase in the inflation rate (a little more than 4 percent annually), so they are preparing to save $22,000 for each year of their daughter's college, which equals $88,000 for the four years.

What if inflation, over the next eight years, is higher than 4 percent? What if inflation is 5 percent or 10 percent during one or two years of that eight-year period? When it comes time to go to school, the Millers' daughter will have a big decision to make. She will not have enough money to cover all four years of college. She might have to take out loans or get a job at the same time she is going to school. If the inflation rate was really high, she might not be able to attend that school at all.

When high inflation hits the economy, the money that people have been saving is no longer worth as much as they had hoped. The money they have saved buys fewer goods and services. During periods of high inflation, people tend to stop buying things like new cars, computers, televisions, houses, and furniture. They usually stop going out to eat in restaurants. They cannot afford to go on vacation or travel to their grandmother's house for Thanksgiving. They stop using the money they have for any extra treats or splurges. They must save their money so they can afford the things that are necessary, such as food, clothing, and home heating. When people stop

Money that you put into a savings account at a bank will be worth less when you take it out in ten years if there has been a steady rise in inflation during that time.

making purchases, stores suffer financially, as do the businesses that make the goods or offer the services. If inflation is too high, businesses might be forced to cut jobs or even shut down and close up shop completely.

So, inflation can be both helpful and harmful. These are just some ways that inflation affects people's lives and businesses. Although low inflation can be beneficial to a country's economy, high inflation can hurt almost everyone. Trying to keep inflation under control is a complicated job as will be seen in the next chapter. The task is further complicated by the fact that inflationary forces are complex. They can't all be controlled by a government department, no matter how powerful. A vast multitude of factors and trends—large and small, major and minor—determine the upward or downward movement of the economy. The government has only a few blunt tools with which to service the incredibly complex and delicate machine that is the national and global economy.

MYTHS and FACTS

MYTH   All inflation is bad.

FACT   Not all inflation is bad. Inflation can stimulate the economy. Inflation sometimes provides extra money for companies, as well as for their employees. When companies have extra money, they can share their profits with their workers. They can also use that money to develop better products.

MYTH   When an economy is experiencing inflation, it means prices for all goods and services are rising.

FACT   This is not necessarily true. Inflation might mean that some products and services have increased in price, while prices for other products and services remain the same or even decrease. Also, some prices for products and services might be rising, but the products and services might have new value-added features (like DVD players in new cars or a new window-washing service added to a standard house-cleaning job) that account for at least some of the price increase. A period of inflation features price increases for a large number of—but not necessarily all—popular goods and services over an extended period of time.

MYTH   Higher inflation means higher wages.

FACT   Just because the economy is experiencing inflation
does not mean that workers will receive higher wages
to keep up with that inflation. Sometimes, company
owners can't afford to increase the wages of their
workers, even if inflation has helped the company
owners to earn bigger profits. During an inflationary
period, company owners often have to pay higher
prices for the materials and services that they have
to buy in order to keep their companies in business.
This leaves them with less money with which to offer
raises to their employees.

CHAPTER FIVE

Controlling Inflation

In 2008, in England, a banking museum displayed computer-simulated models that sought to explain how managing inflation worked. One of the models invited visitors to use a computer simulator to control the flight of a balloon. The visitor was instructed to increase or decrease the air in the balloon to make it either rise or fall. By controlling the inflation and deflation of the balloon, the visitor kept the balloon on a steady course.

Using Interest Rates to Control Inflation

This simulated balloon flight was the museum's way of showing how banking officials try to control inflation in the economy. In the United States, the interest rates that banks use are determined by the Federal Reserve. The Federal Reserve, under the direction of the U.S. Congress, regulates (sets the rules for) many of the banks in the country. One of the major roles of the Federal Reserve is to decide which

The Federal Reserve in Washington, D.C., controls the interest rates charged by banks in the United States.

interest rates banks can charge when they offer loans. As seen earlier, the interest rate is the profit that a bank makes when someone borrows money.

When inflation is high, one of the usual causes is that there is too much money circulating in the marketplace. During inflationary periods, people have a lot of money and the demand for goods and services is very high, though the supply is low. When 100 people want to buy one glass of lemonade, in other words, Scott could probably ask $20 for the glass and receive it because so many people want that glass of lemonade.

Often, the reason there is a lot of money circulating in the market is because interest rates that banks charge are very low. When interest rates are low, people are encouraged to borrow money to buy things that they want. If you wanted to buy a computer game that cost $50 and all you had was $20, you might make a deal with a friend to borrow the extra $30 that you need. You might tell your friend that instead of just paying her back the $30, you will pay back $31. In this way, your friend can make $1 without doing anything, except lending you the money. So, she might agree to the deal. The one extra dollar that you have to pay her will not be that difficult for you. So, you go buy the computer game, and in a month, you pay back the $31.

When bank interest rates are low, it is a good time for people to buy big-ticket items, like houses or cars. This is because they can borrow money from the bank at a low rate. When a lot of people are looking for houses to buy and not that many houses are for sale, then the price of houses rises, or become inflated.

When the Federal Reserve sees that inflation is rising, it raises interest rates. Where interest rates for borrowing money might have been at 5 percent a year, the Federal Reserve might

When interest rates are high, people take out fewer loans and put off major purchases, like cars and houses. House prices may begin to fall as a result of the lower demand.

raise the rate to 7 percent. Whereas a lot of people might have been able to afford a loan at 5 percent, when the interest rates reach 7 percent or more, fewer people can afford to take out a loan. This is because it will be more expensive to pay back that loan. A $100,000 loan with a 5 percent annual interest rate would cost $125,000 to pay back in five years, while a 7 percent interest rate would boost that total to $135,000, $10,000 more than the loan at 5 percent interest. When interest rates rise, therefore, the demand for loans, as well as the demand for new houses, begins to decrease. When the demand decreases, prices fall, as does inflation.

Using credit cards is similar to taking out a bank loan. Interest rates on a credit card also rise and fall. When the rates are low, people use credit cards to buy new washing machines, televisions, DVD players, and other expensive items. Some people use credit cards to pay for airline tickets and hotels when they go on vacations. However, when interest rates are high,

Credit cards are a great convenience, but piling up crushing credit card debt is easy to do and very dangerous for your long-term financial health.

consumers might find that it is very difficult to pay off their credit card debt.

When consumers see how much they have to pay to get out from under their credit card debt, they would be wise to

stop buying goods and services until their debt is paid off. If a lot of people are in debt, and they use their money to pay off their bills instead of buying new products, then the demand for goods and services diminishes. And as you know by now, that means prices should begin to fall and inflationary pressures will decrease. If prices and spending levels fall too low, the Federal Reserve may lower interest rates to encourage borrowing and spending and kick-start the slowing economy. These lower rates would make it easier to obtain money, as well as easier to pay down debt at lower interest.

Using Increases in Wages to Control Inflation

Inflation is not felt as deeply when workers' wages keep up

61

with the inflation rate. So when workers notice that the paychecks they bring home are no longer enough to pay for their house, food, and clothing, they might go to their bosses and ask for more money.

This father and daughter search hard for a reasonably priced loaf of bread. During periods of inflation, people find themselves putting a lot of careful thought into purchases that used to be unremarkable.

When salaries keep up with inflation, when they get higher as inflation gets higher, then increases in wages help to control inflation. Although inflation continues to rise, so, too, do workers' salaries, so no financial pain is felt.

The Bottom Line on Inflation

If inflation is controlled, it can stimulate the economy and provide profits for businesses and raises in wages for workers. However, if inflation is not controlled, it can send prices so high that buying a loaf of bread can be as dramatic an event as buying a car is now.

Keeping inflation at a reasonable rate is partially the responsibility of the Federal Reserve, which sets the interest rates for banks. Yet, it is individual Americans, in their role as consumers, who perhaps have an even more crucial role in influencing the heating up or cooling down of the economy. When inflation gets too high, people stop buying goods and services that they do not really need. As the demand for goods and services drops, prices usually also drop.

In the end, inflation is neither all good nor all bad. It has its benefits and its dangers. One thing that is for certain, however, is that it is here to stay. Navigating the upward swells of inflation and the sudden plummets of deflation, riding the big waves of a swelling and crashing economy, can be a scary thrill ride. It requires a calm mind, a cool head, and careful planning. If you are smart with your money by, for example, always saving a part of your paycheck in a fund to be used only in times of economic emergency, you will have a sense of security and the reassuring knowledge that you can ride out whatever economic rough waters have been stirred up. You do not have to be a helpless victim of the economy's ups and downs. Instead, you can manage and spend your money wisely, invest it prudently, and save it carefully. You can protect yourself from the uncertainty and panic that often grips the markets and focus instead on calmly enjoying your security and planning for the future and the kind of life you would like to create for yourself.

Ten Great Questions
to Ask an Economist

1. How much will college cost when I am old enough to attend?

2. If inflation continues at the same rate as today, what kinds of salaries can I expect to earn in different jobs in the future?

3. What is the rate of inflation today? What was the rate of inflation when my grandparents were my age?

4. I have a small amount of money to invest to eventually help pay for college. Given the current rate of inflation and the economy, and considering likely future trends, where is the best place to put this money? What option would offer the best return on my investment? Which is the safest option, the one that would prevent a loss on my investment?

5. What is happening in the economy today? Are we experiencing inflation or deflation?

6. When the U. S. economy is experiencing inflation, are all the other countries in the world also experiencing inflation?

7. Which is better for an economy, inflation or deflation?

Ten Great Questions
to Ask an Economist

8 When the economy is experiencing an inflation that continues to increase, is it a good idea to buy things now when the prices are lower even if we can't afford them?

9 I have some money saved in the bank. But the interest I earn is only 2 percent. If the inflation rate is at 3 percent, aren't I losing money?

10 My parents told me that, because of inflation, our house is worth more today than it was ten years ago when they bought it. But our three-year-old car is worth less. Why is this?

GLOSSARY

barter To trade goods or services without the exchange of money.

commodity An article of trade or commerce, especially an agricultural or mining product that can be processed and resold.

consumer price index (CPI) A measurement of the prices of goods and services bought by consumers. It is used to gauge inflation.

cost-push inflation Persistent increase in prices that results from higher production costs that are then reflected in the price of products.

currency Money in any form that is used as a medium of exchange, especially circulating paper money.

deflation A persistent decrease in the level of consumer prices.

demand-pull inflation Persistent increase in prices that results from an increase in the demand for goods and services by households, the government, businesses, or foreign countries.

devalue To lessen the value of something; to lower the exchange value.

economics The study of economy.

economy A careful management of resources, such as money, and the system of economic activity in a country.

Federal Reserve The central controlling bank of the United States that sets the laws by which all other U.S. banks function.

fixed income Revenue that remains constant, regardless of changing economic factors such as inflation.

goods and services Things that people buy. Goods, like television sets or cars, are tangible objects that are purchased and used by the consumer. Services, like haircuts or house cleaning, are things that are done for you when you pay for them.

hyperinflation Extremely high inflation or inflation that is out of control.

inflation A general increase in the prices of goods and services over a period of time.

interest rate The rate that a bank charges when a person takes out a loan.

market basket A group of almost 80,000 popular goods and services used to calculate the consumer price index.

profits The money that a business makes after all the bills are paid.

purchasing (or buying) power The amount of goods and services that a dollar can buy.

reinvest To put money back into a business or an investment commodity.

FOR MORE INFORMATION

Board of Governors of the Federal Reserve System
20th Street and Constitution Avenue NW
Washington, DC 20551
Web site: http://www.federalreserve.gov/default.htm
The Federal Reserve System is the central bank of the United
States. The Federal Reserve's duties include conducting the
nation's monetary policy, supervising and regulating banking
institutions, maintaining the stability of the financial system,
and providing financial services to depository institutions, the
U.S. government, and foreign official institutions.

Bureau of Labor Statistics (BLS)
Division of Information Services
2 Massachusetts Avenue NE, Room 2860
Washington, DC 20212
(202) 691-5200
(800) 877-8339
Web site: http://www.bls.gov
The Bureau of Labor Statistics is the principal fact-finding
agency for the federal government in the broad field of
labor economics and statistics. The BLS is an independent
national statistical agency that collects, processes, analyzes,
and disseminates essential statistical data to the American
public, the U.S. Congress, other federal agencies, state and

local governments, business, and labor. The BLS also serves as a statistical resource to the Department of Labor.

Department of Finance Canada
19th floor, East Tower
140 O'Connor Street
Ottawa, ON K1A 0G5
Canada
(613) 992-1573
The Department of Finance Canada is the federal department primarily responsible for providing the government of Canada with analysis and advice on the broad economic and financial affairs of the country. Its responsibilities include preparing the federal budget, preparing tax and tariff legislation, managing federal borrowing on financial markets, developing regulatory policy for the financial sector, and representing Canada within international financial institutions.

National Council on Economic Education (NCEE)
1140 Avenue of the Americas
New York, NY 10036
(212) 730-7007
(800) 338-1192
Web site: http://www.ncee.net
NCEE offers comprehensive programs that equip teachers with tools to get economics and personal finance into the classroom, and to help students apply in their lives what they learn in school.

Statistics Canada
100 Tunney's Pasture Driveway

Ottawa, ON K1A 0T6
Canada
(800) 263-1136
Web site: http://www.statcan.ca/start.html
Statistics Canada produces statistics that help Canadians better
    understand their country—its population, resources, economy,
    society, and culture.

U.S. Department of the Treasury
1500 Pennsylvania Avenue NW
Washington, DC 20220
(202) 622-2000
Web site: http://www.ustreas.gov
The Treasury Department is the executive agency responsible
    for promoting economic prosperity and ensuring the financial
    security of the United States. The department is responsible
    for a wide range of activities, such as advising the president
    on economic and financial issues, encouraging sustainable
    economic growth, and fostering improved governance in
    financial institutions. The Department of the Treasury operates
    and maintains systems that are critical to the nation's financial
    infrastructure, such as the production of coins and currency,
    the disbursement of payments to the American public, revenue
    collection, and the borrowing of funds necessary to run the
    federal government.

U.S. Mint
Office of Public Affairs
801 9th Street NW
Washington, DC 20220-0001
Web site: http://www.usmint.gov

The primary mission of the United States Mint is to produce an adequate volume of circulating coinage for the nation to conduct its trade and commerce. In addition to producing coins, the United States Mint has other responsibilities, including distributing U.S. coins to the Federal Reserve banks and branches, maintaining physical custody and protection of the nation's $100 billion gold and silver assets, and manufacturing and selling platinum, gold, and silver bullion coins.

Web sites

Due to the changing nature of Internet links, Rosen Publishing has developed an online list of Web sites related to the subject of this book. This site is updated regularly. Please use this link to access this list:

http://www.rosenlinks.com/rwe/infl

FOR FURTHER READING

Adil, Janeen R. *Goods and Services* (First Facts). Mankato, MN: Capstone Press, 2006.

Adil, Janeen R. *Scarcity* (First Facts). Mankato, MN: Capstone Press, 2006.

Adil, Janeen R. *Supply and Demand* (First Facts). Mankato, MN: Capstone Press, 2006.

Allman, Barbara. *Banking* (How Economics Works). Minneapolis, MN: Lerner, 2005.

Blatt, Jessica. *The Teen Girl's Gotta-Have-It Guide to Money: Getting Smart About Making It, Saving It, and Spending It!* (Teen Girl's Gotta-Have-It Guides). New York, NY: Watson-Guptill, 2007.

Cribb, Joe, and Laura Bullen. *Money*. New York, NY: DK Children, 2005.

Davis, James E., Phyllis Maxey Fernlund, and Peter Woll. *Civics: Government and Economics in Action*. Upper Saddle River, NJ: Prentice Hall, 2005.

Gali, Jordi. *Monetary Policy, Inflation, and the Business Cycle: An Introduction to the New Keynesian Framework*. Princeton, NJ: Princeton University Press, 2008.

Gilman, Laura Anne. *Economics* (How Economics Works). Minneapolis, MN: Lerner, 2006.

Hall, Alvin. *Show Me the Money: How to Make Cents of Economics*. New York, NY: DK Publishing, 2008.

Harman, Hollis Page. *Money Sense for Kids*. Hauppauge, NY: Barron's Educational Series, 2005.

Hazlitt, Henry. *What You Should Know About Inflation*. Auburn, AL: Ludwig von Mises Institute, 2007.

Holyoke, Nancy. *A Smart Girl's Guide to Money: How to Make It, Save It, and Spend It* (American Girl Library). Middleton, WI: American Girl Publishing, Inc., 2006.

McGraw-Hill. *Civics Today: Citizenship, Economics, and You, Student Edition*. New York, NY: Glencoe/ McGraw-Hill, 2006.

McGraw-Hill. *Economics: Today and Tomorrow, Student Edition*. New York, NY: Glencoe/McGraw-Hill, 2007.

O'Sullivan, Arthur, and Steven M. Sheffrin. *Economics: Principles in Action*. Upper Saddle River, NJ: Pearson Prentice Hall, 2006.

Steinberg, Ed, et al. *The Story of Inflation*. New York, NY: The Federal Reserve Bank of New York, 2007.

BIBLIOGRAPHY

Ball, R.J. *Inflation and the Theory of Money*. Piscataway, NJ: Aldine Transaction, 2007.

Bank of England Museum. "The Pound in Your Pocket Exhibition." Retrieved September 2008 (http://www.bankofengland.co.uk/education/museum/exhibitions/current.htm).

Bureau of Labor Statistics. "Inflation and Prices." U.S. Department of Labor. Retrieved September 2008 (http://www.bls.gov/data/).

Davies, Glyn, and Roy Davies. *A History of Money from Ancient Times to the Present Day*. Cardiff, Wales: University of Wales Press, 2002.

Ferguson, Niall. *The Ascent of Money: A Financial History of the World*. New York, NY: Penguin Press, 2008.

Hanes, Chris. "Prices and Price Indices." *Historical Statistics of the United States*. Edited by Susan B. Carter, Scott S. Gartner, Michael Haines, Alan L. Olmstead, Richard Sutch, and Gavin Wright. New York, NY: Cambridge University Press, 2002.

McGreal, Chris. "What Comes After a Trillion: Inflation in Zimbabwe." *The Guardian*. July 18, 2008, p. 12.

Mishkin, Frederic S. *Monetary Policy Strategy*. Cambridge, MA: MIT Press, 2007.

Nova. "The History of Money." PBS.org, August 2002. Retrieved September 2008 (http://www.pbs.org/wgbh/nova/moolah/history.html).

Salvatore, Dominich, and Eugene Diulio. *Principles of Economics.* New York, NY: McGraw Hill, 2008.

Samuelson, Robert J. *The Great Inflation and Its Aftermath: The Past and Future of American Affluence.* New York, NY: Random House, 2008.

Swaneberg, August. *Macroeconomics DeMystified.* New York, NY: McGraw-Hill, 2005.

INDEX

About the Author

Joyce Hart is a writer who has watched inflation affect the rising cost of tuition, from the time of her own undergraduate years to the present day, when her children are all currently attending college. Inflation has helped her because the cost and value of her home has risen over the years, giving her a good return on her investment. Inflation has also hurt, however, as the price of food and gasoline has become far more expensive. She lives outside of Seattle, Washington, and must take a ferry to go to the city. Every year, the cost of the ferry ride goes up. To control the inflation of her personal expenses, she now travels to Seattle no more than once a month.

Photo Credits

Cover (top) © www.istockphoto.com/Andrey Prokhorov; cover (bottom) © www.istockphoto.com/Lilli Day; p. 1 © Mario Tama/Getty Images; pp. 6–7, 14, 40–41 © Joe Raedle/Getty Images; pp. 8, 16, 19 © Justin Sullivan/Getty Images; p. 11 © Spencer Platt/Getty Images; p. 21 British Library, London, UK/The Bridgeman Art Library; p. 23 © Bruno Vincent/Getty Images; p. 26 © HIP/Art Resource; pp. 28–29 www.istockphoto.com; p. 30 Anthony Potter Collection/Getty Images; pp. 32–33, 39, 59, 62–63 © AP Photos; p. 37 © Chris Hondros/Getty Images; pp. 42–43 © Getty Images; pp. 46–47 © Rick Gershon/Getty Images; pp. 48–49 © Shutterstock; pp. 52–53 © Bill Aron/Photo Edit; p. 57 Karen Bleier/Getty Images; pp. 60–61 © Newscom.

Designer: Sam Zavieh; Photo Researcher: Marty Levick